Questions

for

My Father

Questions for My Father

My Father

Finding the Man Behind Your Dad

Vincent Staniforth

BEYOND
WORDS
Publishing
I N C

Beyond Words Publishing, Inc.
20827 N.W. Cornell Road, Suite 500
Hillsboro, Oregon 97124-9808
503-531-8700 · 1-800-284-9673

Editor: Marvin Moore
Cover and interior design: Richard Cohn and Fran Lee

Printed in the United States of America by Publishers Press
Distributed to the book trade by Publishers Group West

Library of Congress Cataloging-in-Publication Data
Staniforth, Vincent, 1960-
    Questions for my father : finding the man behind your dad /
Vincent Staniforth.

        p. cm.
    ISBN 1-885223-74-9
    1. Fathers and sons. I. Title.
HQ756.S74 1998
306.874'2—dc21   97-49136
                                                                            CIP

The corporate mission of Beyond Words Publishing, Inc.:
Inspire to Integrity

For

John Staniforth
and for my
sun and moon—
John Harley
and Conor David Edmund

Introduction

This book is the result of long midnight conversations with Dad—but they were conversations that took place in the dreams and quiet, troubled times in the years following his death. While I remember his answers to a few of these questions from his living years, for the rest I can only wish that he was around in person so I could hear his response without the unreliable filter of memory or interpretation.

This book may prompt dads and their children to ask each other these and many other questions. Or it may prompt dads to think of how their own fathers might have responded. But these are *my* questions, and by asking them I've recalled things Dad said and did that I would never have remembered had I not committed them to paper. While originally written with my own dad—and later, all dads—in mind, most of these questions can be addressed to both parents and can be asked by either a son or a daughter. The underlying objective, however, has been to develop a blueprint for discovery so that children of any age can build a clearer, deeper picture of the man behind the word *Dad*.

You could easily ask a set of questions completely different from mine, questions as urgent or as playful as those in the following pages. I was fortunate. I didn't have to ask any of the darker, angry questions that children sometimes have to ask; I assumed that all fathers were as constant and godlike as mine. Even so, Dad and I never talked about many of these questions and topics, and I don't want the same thing to happen to me and my sons. I want us to talk openly and deeply to each other—often—and I want to hear them ask many other questions, too.

I had ample opportunity to ask these questions, and the few times we talked candidly revealed in much more detail the beautiful man I knew my father was. Which makes my neglect of that relationship all the more painful. A million reasons not to ask these questions could always be found. It was a waste of all the things Dad had ever seen and done not to hear his answers, and I regret not finding out more about him when I had the chance.

So this is for my dad. And for all dads past, present, and future. And for their sons and daughters. And for the simple pleasure of talking to each other.

What's the most important
lesson you learned from your dad?

Who was your first love?

What's your biggest regret?

$\mathcal{A}$s a boy,
what did you want to be
when you grew up?

$\mathcal{W}$hat was your happiest
teenage day?

$\mathcal{D}$o you find yourself

saying

the same things to me

that your dad

said to you?

How did you learn about
the facts of life?

What's it like having

grown-up
children?

What does
God
mean to you?

*I*t's important for children to allow their father to be seen as fallible, if only sometimes. As a teenager, I felt I was immeasurably wiser and savvier than my dad. But as I grew older, I saw my dad as more of a man, because he let me share in some of his fears and regrets. Because of that courage in showing me that he was just another guy, I saw him even more as godlike and supremely lovable.

What's your secret for making
a woman smile?

Do you ever think about
your mom and dad?

Where and what do you think
I'll be when I'm seventy?

Do you ever think
about death?

I was talking with two old friends one evening about losing our fathers.

"We're part of a club," I said, "and everyone joins it sooner or later.

"We were lucky. We didn't have to subscribe till we were in our thirties. Some people join it from birth."

And so we raised our glasses to a toast of Making Every Second Count with our children.

$\mathcal{H}$ow will I know when I've
met my true love?

$\mathcal{S}$hould I strive to be happy,
or strive to be successful?

$\mathcal{W}$hat's the biggest mistake you've ever
made? What can I learn from it?

How should I deal
with hard times?

What makes a good dad?

What makes a good
son or daughter?

What happened on your
favorite holiday?

Have you ever regretted
having children?

How does a dad get through
his children's adolescence?

What has influenced and formed
your political thinking?

Are sports important?
How?

What's your favorite movie?

What did you feel
the first time
you cradled me
in your arms?

Should marriage really
mean *forever*?

Which is your favorite season?
Why?

Did you have to kill anyone
in the war?
Do you ever think about
those experiences?

A young man stands in the deep night of the jungle. He's at war, he's carrying a rifle, and he's scared.

Forty years later, another youth stands in a city with a checkbook in hand, just starting out in business, and scared.

Which one has more courage? I always thought that even if I lived through a dozen recessions, it still wouldn't be the same as having to go through a war like my dad. But he saw it differently, saying, "You're growing up in a different world. I wouldn't survive having to do what your generation has to do. They don't give out medals for getting up every morning and feeding a family.

"But that's what real guts is all about."

What's your favorite book?
Why?

Where were you when man
first set foot on the moon?

How would you feel
if I wanted to be
an artist or poet?

*H*ow did you deal
with your dad's death?

Coming to terms with my dad's death
did not come easily to me.
I once complained to my wife that it
just didn't seem fair that my dad had died
when I was only thirty.

"I think you need to look at it another way,"
she said. "You had him for thirty whole years."

And the cloud vanished.
I saw myself as blessed, instead of
unfairly treated.
Maybe we need to instill this viewpoint in our
children. Moms and dads are finite resources.
However long we have them needs to be
the best time possible.
And I remember that comment
every time I pick up the phone
to talk to Mom.

What did you always want
to do but never had the
chance?

What's your own
Golden Rule?

Questions to Ask My Children

What should it mean
when someone says,
"I love you"?

What's the biggest risk
you've ever taken?

How will I know when a risk
is worth taking?

What's the most important thing to
remember about money?

What did you want me to
be when I grew up?

What's the mark
of a good person?

Is mankind born
good or bad?

What do you love most
about this country?

If I'm in love with two women,
how do I know which to choose?

*C*an a man and a woman
find lasting happiness?

*H*ow hard should I pursue
my dreams?

What's the worst part
about growing older?

Life is unpredictable—
what's the best way
to handle its surprises?

What would your advice be
if I were drafted to go to war?

What's the biggest difference
between raising sons and daughters?

Which is more important
to study,
art or science?

What should I do when
someone wrongs me?

Is my life already determined,
or am I in control of my destiny?

Who has been your
best friend?

What makes a real friend?

I remember clearly, as do my
brother and sisters,
the delight we felt when our parents
used to tell us stories
about their childhood days.
What is it about imagining Dad
as a young boy that was so
mesmerising?

What's your most
vivid memory
of your mom and dad?

How will I know when
I'm successful?

*I*s it possible to be a complete adult without suffering hardship, adversity, or danger?

What do you believe happens
when we die?

In a world of compromises,
how do I keep true to myself?

What's the best part of
having a son?

Two minutes before a soccer match when I was seven, my bootlace snapped. While I fell apart, my dad calmly knelt and repaired the lace, softly saying, "Better it happened here than out on the field."

As young as I was, I thought it was a pretty amazing thing to say. As I grew up, I remember thinking how unlikely it would be that I would ever be as wise as my dad. Then, just recently, my own six-year-old son's bootlace snapped before a soccer game, and as I tied the lace while he fretted, I casually told him that it was better that this kind of thing happen on the sidelines rather than in the action. He agreed, and ran off happily to play his game.

As I watched, I realized that I'd just become conspirator in the Great Dad Pact—the secret game that all fathers play where we pretend to be the source of great wisdom that, in fact, we have merely inherited and made our own.

Is that so bad?

No, I think it's great that my sons, at this young age, can believe that whatever problems the world presents, Mom and Dad can fix them. There will be time enough in later years to see that it isn't so all the time. What I should have told him was that my dad did exactly the same thing for me and that it was all part of being a dad and of loving someone.

How will I know when I've found the
right place to put down roots?

What's the biggest
difference between my world
and the world you grew up in?

How did you propose to Mom?

What were the key events
that changed your life?

Where would you most like to
visit in the world?
Why?

What's the good part
about getting older?

How did it feel to let me go
to make my own life?

How can I make each
of my children feel as if
they're the most special?

How do I become

my own person

rather than the man

society says I should be?

Who do you admire the most?
Why?

Have you found it possible
to forgive people
who wronged you?

How will I know when to keep quiet
and when to speak my mind?

What do you think has been
your greatest achievement?

If you could go back and change
one event in your life,
what would it be
and how would you change it?

*I*s it better to be self-reliant
or to develop a network of friends
to call upon for help?

*D*o you think you're a
contented man?

*W*hat should I do when I'm angry
with my children?

I've learned so much from what I believe
my dad did right in his life.
I've also learned a lot from reflecting
    on the mistakes he made.
And when I get smug about being able to
develop my parent skills by learning
    from another's mistakes,
I suddenly realize that my boys will learn
from my mistakes.
                Scary.

What did you like most—
and least—
about your dad?

Have you ever carried
a long-term grudge
against someone?
Why?

Have you ever had to do
something that took
a lot of courage?
What happened?

What was the funniest thing
you ever saw your children do?

Can you remember your parents
laughing? What was the cause?

What do you wish
you'd asked your dad?

*D*ads can be multidimensional
mystery characters.
Is it because they withhold so much,
or is it because
we don't ask the right questions?

Do you think you spent too much time at work when we were young?

Do you think you were too strict with your children?

Did you and Mom carefully plan how to raise us, or did you improvise?

If you could change
one thing about me,
what would it be?

What do you remember
about my character
as a young child?

What's your favorite
song of all time?
What or who does
it remind you of?

What's the best time of
life for a man?

What has been your proudest day as a dad?

Looking back through
your dad, granddad,
and so on,
what characteristic
do we all share?

What have you learned
from being a dad?

I'm not a perfect dad. I'm very far from it.
But I believe with all my heart that
I can be a better dad.
Can I be a better dad
than my own father?
We'll see—
but I'll do my best
to make sure that my children
will know me more completely
than I knew my dad,
and that's a start.

Have you kept secrets from
Mom during your marriage?
To protect you or her?

Have you ever
faced total despair?
What did you do?

What are your guiding
principles for doing business?

What were parties like
when you were
a young man?

What is a dad's primary
role—teacher, protector,
provider, pal, or disciplinarian?

How is my style of fatherhood
different from yours?

What do you think has been the
number one cause of our arguments?

What makes
a good daughter?

Do you fear more for
a son or a daughter
as they face
the outside world?

*H*ow have you wanted
your children
to think of you?

*H*ow do you ask these questions without
creating an awkward moment?
Maybe that's the problem.
We've gotten out of the habit of having
meaningful conversations.
One of the casualties of our time is that the
people who should matter the most
are the ones we often take for granted.

$\mathcal{D}$id you ever feel complete anger
and frustration at your children?
How did you deal with it?

$\mathcal{H}$ow does the role of
a dad and a mom differ?

$\mathcal{W}$hat would you change
about your style of fathering?

$\mathcal{H}$ow did you and Mom keep
your relationship alive
while raising a family?

$\mathcal{D}$id you enjoy
being single?

Who first broke your heart?
What happened?

What makes you proud
to be a man?

Does a man "love" differently
than a woman?

Is there such a thing as
a "right" war?

All things considered,
would you rather have grown up
in your world or
in today's world?

Did being a dad come naturally?

What causes racial
or religious prejudice?

What makes a good
spouse?

Are you frightened
of anything now?

Is there anything you've
always wanted to ask me?

How old do you feel today?

Should I live
with my mistakes or always
try to cut my losses and
make a clean start?

Did your parents have
favorites? Did you?

If you were a young man today,
would you have a family again?

Define family.

Define a life well lived.

What's the best part of
having a daughter?

When I was born,
what was your
dream for me?

Questions to Ask My Dad

What are the vital ingredients of a strong marriage?

What's
your favorite memory
of spending time with me?

What did you worry
about most as
I was growing up?

How did you meet Mom?
Where did you go
on your first date?

How long did you know each
other before you got married?

What was your
wedding day like?

What would you do if something happened to Mom?

What did you always want
to do with your kids
but never had the chance?

Were you ever tempted to
just walk away from your
family responsibilities?

*H*ow have you
remotivated yourself
when faced with
bad times?

What was the greatest gift your parents gave you? Have you tried to instill the same lessons in your children? Do you think you succeeded?

Should I try to retain
an idealistic worldview
or adopt
a more pragmatic view?

When did you get your first car?
What model was it?

Did you go as far
academically
as you wanted?

What was your
happiest school day?

What was your first job?

When you were
growing up,
did you hope to be a
father someday?

Afterword

These questions should have been asked when Dad was alive. They remained unasked for many reasons: lack of time, lack of nerve in some cases (*Will he be offended if I ask him this question?*), lack of courage in others (*Do I really want to know the answer to that question?*). But they remained lodged in my head because of a fierce desire, growing stronger as I matured (slowly), to know—truly know—my dad. For me, as I suspect is the case with many men and women, that desire for knowledge seemed to burn brightest just before the extinction of the source of its energy. My realization of how much more I wanted to learn about my dad came so clearly that I can still recall the moment.

It's a rainy afternoon in Telluride, Colorado, in mid-September 1990. A married man of nearly three weeks, I am honeymooning on a cross-country motorcycle trip from Atlanta to San Francisco. Ominous, piling clouds have been chasing us down these mountain roads all morning. Cold and wet, we decide to stop in this town for the night and revive ourselves with coffee and brandy at a bar on the main street.

Viv, my wife, goes exploring while I order another brandy with hot water and mull over the notes I've been making since we left Atlanta. These scribbles are comments on what we've seen, the people we've met, the minor hitches and laughs that make up any travelogue, but I begin to notice that as we've travelled farther down the road, my notes are becoming more abstract, less literal. My notes talk about how it feels to be married (no surprise there), and I imagine how Mom and Dad started their life together in 1947; I comment on the enormity and uncertainty of this bike ride—we're a long way from our home in England—and try to imagine how Dad thought about his own long journey as an infantryman in Burma in World War II.

Taking my pen, I begin to write; I ask myself to imagine what it must have been like for my parents to let me go and begin to live my own life. On another motorcycle, on another rainy day a long time ago, I see Dad waving from the kitchen window as I leave to ride to college. How did that feel for him? Then I ask them what it's like having grown-up children. I wish more than anything else that Dad was beside me at this bar so we could talk and talk and he could tell me much more about who he is.

According to my watch, it's 2:30 p.m. Mountain Time, which puts England at 9:30 p.m. A map of the United States hangs over the breakfast bar of my parents' kitchen, and not for the first time during this ride I become very sure that right now he's looking at the map and tracing our route, wondering if we're safe, and looking forward to our return. Looking in the mirror behind the bar in Telluride, I get the eerie but not uncomfortable feeling that Dad is looking back at me from the other side. I wish he were here. I have a terrible feeling of time slipping through my fingers.

Ten days later, back in Atlanta and getting ready to fly home to England, I took a call telling me that Dad had had a stroke. The next day, jet-lagged and disbelieving, I sat next to him as he fought the stroke that had taken his consciousness and was relentlessly battering him toward death. The youngest of his five children sharing the long hours of vigil, I sat alone with him in the empty hours of the morning and recounted events from the motorcycle trip in the hope that he could still hear and understand a familiar voice. Stories poured out of me about our adventures and the times I'd thought so vividly about him in places like Memphis, Boulder, the Grand Canyon, Telluride, and Big Sur. But Dad was unconscious and gave no sign of recognition beyond a small flicker of his fingers when I first held his hand. He died a couple of hours later.

In the years following his death, I came to see just how much I had failed to learn from

Dad—and about Dad. Certainly, he'd bestowed upon me the broad strokes, the crucial guidelines and directives that shaped me and continue to shape me—and my two sons—even today. I knew I was loved. He knew I loved him. But there was so much more there. All that time, all I ever had to do was ask the questions. But they remained unasked, and so all I have today is memory, conjecture, interpretation, and a determination that my children won't know this kind of frustration. So the questions and ideas that Dad and I addressed in my dreams and in those solitary, quiet moments were put to paper. Over time, the list grew and grew. It was therapy, a way of coping with his death. It was good to talk to Dad again.

One day in 1996, I was sitting in a bagel shop, laboring over an early draft of this book, when two women noticed the papers spread out before me and asked what the questions were about. After I explained the idea behind the book, one of them exclaimed, "Oh, neat!" and began leafing through a couple of pages. The second woman said, "You know, I'd use this to start talking to my dad. All we do is argue. I can just sit him down at Thanksgiving and start asking him this stuff." The first woman put the sheaf of papers back on the table and added, "But where are the answers?" I replied that I'd been asking the same question since my dad died. After they left, her comment echoed again and again, giving me doubts about the whole project. Why, I asked myself, in a culture that spoon-feeds information and products to consumers each and every day, would anyone be interested in reading a stream of questions without having recourse to an index of answers? I almost left that draft in the trash can.

Instead, the book continued to develop, and gradually I saw the woman's question as the absolute essence of why the book needed to see publication. The very fact that there are no answers within these covers focuses the reader on the questions. No one can repeat any question to themselves without formulating some kind of reply, however abstract or abrupt. There was a need, I believed, to put such questions down on paper and use them as a blueprint to uncover more about the man behind the word *Dad*.

My encounter with the women in the bagel shop also made me see the book in another light; so far, I'd been approaching the idea from my own particular circumstance, i.e., my dad had died and these were questions that I wished I had asked him when he was still alive. But what about those people who want to learn more about their fathers who are still living? What about fathers who want to talk about these questions and issues, unbidden, to their children? What about children who want to know more about their father's relationship with his father? The book seemed to be offering a proto-map of discovery not only of the father figure but also of the reader. It was offering a way—sometimes playful, sometimes serious—to let fathers tell their stories and to make children, young or old, explore their own knowledge and understanding of their dad. And if that knowledge and understanding simply does not exist—for whatever reason—the questions then turn around and shine an inquiring light onto the reader: *How do I think my dad might have answered this question? How do I think I might answer the same question to my children?*

Considering these questions, you might come to agree with the view that this book is

more about self-discovery than dad-discovery.
And finally, I want to emphasize that these are
my questions. I urge you to develop your own
questions. Sit down with your dad—even if he's
not around—and ask him your questions. Sit
down with your children and answer the same
questions. Make your own discovery. We have to
stop being afraid of asking questions. And we
have to start being brave enough to listen
to the answers.

Notes

Notes

Other Books from Beyond Words Publishing, Inc.

Letters to Our Daughters:
Mothers' Words of Love
Authors: Kristine Van Raden and Molly Davis,
$19.95 hardcover

     Letters to Our Daughters brings together letters from mothers to their daughters from around the world and from all walks of life. What unites these writings is that regardless of life circumstances, education, beliefs, economic status, or age, each mother rejoices in the uniqueness of her daughter and desires for her a future filled with hope, strength, and self-worth. The book includes over forty letters and photos of mothers and daughters who share their stories of courage and triumph, pain and loss, wisdom and love. Touching and inspirational, *Letters to Our Daughters* makes a perfect gift for all women. It can become a cherished keepsake because it provides a place in which the reader can place her own personal letter and photograph. The authors have written an invitation to the reader in which they suggest ways each individual mother can compose her own unique message of love.

Watermelon Magic:
Seeds of Wisdom, Slices of Life
Author: Wally Amos, $14.95 softcover

      Watermelon Magic is an inspirational/motivational book using watermelons as a metaphor for life. Utilizing the life experiences of Wally Amos, the book shows the parallels between watermelons and humans. *Watermelon Magic* tells how Wally Amos uses his faith in everyday life and the wisdom gained from the past to help him make wise choices. Just as the vine connects the watermelons, we are all connected by spirit. And just as prickly vines make it difficult to get the melons, our human connections are sometimes prickly, making it difficult for us to achieve our goals and realize our dreams. *Watermelon Magic* helps us acknowledge the difficulties and choose a path to success.

Hindsights:
The Wisdom and Breakthroughs of Remarkable People
Author: Guy Kawasaki, $22.95 hardcover

What have you learned from your life that you would like to share with the next generation? Get a fresh appreciation of the human experience in this inspirational collection of interviews with thirty-three people who have overcome unique challenges. They are candid about their failures and disappointments, and insightful about turning adversity into opportunity. Guy Kawasaki spent over two years researching and interviewing such people as Apple Computer co-founder Steve Wozniak, management guru Tom Peters, and entrepreneur May Kay. But not everyone in the book is a celebrity. They share their revelations and life experiences, motivating the reader for both personal and professional growth.

You Can Have It All
Author: Arnold M. Patent, $16.95 hardcover

Joy, peace, abundance—these gifts of the Universe are available to each of us whenever we choose to play the real game of life: the game of mutual support. *You Can Have It All* is a guidebook that shows us how to move beyond our beliefs in struggle and shortage, open our hearts, and enjoy a life of true ecstasy. Arnold Patent first self-published *You Can Have It All* in 1984, and it became a classic with over 200,000 copies in print. This revised and expanded edition reflects his greater understanding of the principles and offers practical suggestions as well as simple exercises for improving the quality of our lives.

The Venture Adventure:
Strategies for Thriving in the Jungle of Entrepreneurship
Author: Daryl Bernstein, $12.95 softcover

As traditional entry-level jobs become scarce, today's job-seekers are realizing that if they can't find a job, they can create one. In *The Venture Adventure*, author Daryl Bernstein shows readers how to turn vision into venture capital by creating a business. He uses a jungle-safari metaphor for starting and growing a small business. Daryl's nine "Adventure Principles" will help readers enjoy and benefit from every stage in the journey, make wise decisions when faced with challenges, and reach their destination with enough energy remaining to enjoy the treasure. The reader is engaged on a personal level with suggestions for creating jobs that foster his or her own unique personality. Bernstein's profiles for the hottest business opportunities—including band agenting, coffeehouses, and multimedia publishing—get readers primed to venture out on their own.

Home Sweeter Home:
Creating a Haven of Simplicity and Spirit
Author: Jann Mitchell; Foreword: Jack Canfield.
$12.95 softcover

We search the world for spirituality and peace—only to discover that happiness and satisfaction are not found "out there" in the world but right here in our houses and in our hearts. Award-winning journalist and author Jann Mitchell offers creative insights and suggestions for making our home life more nurturing, spiritual, and rewarding for ourselves, our families, and our friends.

When Money Is Not Enough:
Fulfillment in Work
Author: Eileen R. Hannegan, M.S., $10.95 softcover

In an age when Americans spend more than half their waking hours either at work or performing a function related to work, it is important that the workplace be a healthy community rather than a chaotic battleground. *When Money Is Not Enough* offers the premise that when personality battles create stress and illness, no amount of money in the world is enough to justify continued employment. The book is neither pro-employer nor pro-employee in its approach. Instead, it encourages increasing interdependence among all staff members. Approaching the workplace as a community or family is the key to resolving problems. Drawing from her years of experience as a consultant and lecturer in family systems and organizational development, author Eileen R. Hannegan offers proven methods of transforming the workplace from toxic to healthy. Work can indeed enhance life as well as pay the bills.

Seeing Without Glasses:
Improving Your Vision Naturally
Author: Dr. Robert-Michael Kaplan,
$12.95 softcover; $19.95 hardcover

Seeing Without Glasses invites you to become an active participant in maintaining vision-fitness and preventing eye problems. The premise is stunningly simple: Eye fitness can be developed in exactly the same way other parts of the body are toned—through exercise and diet. Businesses benefit as productivity increases when their employees use preventive techniques to avoid computer eyestrain and to reduce the negative side effects of vision stress. This is a valuable handbook for anyone looking to improve his or her vision or to maintain healthy eyesight.

Rites of Passage:
Celebrating Life's Changes
Authors: Kathleen Wall, Ph.D., and Gary Ferguson.
$12.95 softcover

Every major transition in our lives—be it marriage, high-school graduation, the death of a parent or spouse, or the last child leaving home—brings with it opportunities for growth and self-actualization and for repositioning ourselves in the world. Personal ritual—the focus of *Rites of Passage*—allows us to use the energy held within the anxiety of change to nourish the new person that is forever struggling to be born. *Rites of Passage* begins by explaining to readers that human growth is not linear, as

many of us assume, but rather occurs in a four-part cycle.
After sharing the patterns of transition, the authors then
show the reader how ritual can help him or her move
through these specific life changes: work and career,
intimate relationships, friends, divorce, changes within the
family, adolescence, issues in the last half of life,
and personal loss.

To order or to request a catalog, contact
BEYOND WORDS PUBLISHING, INC.
20827 N.W. Cornell Road, Suite 500
Hillsboro, OR 97124-9808

503-531-8700 or 1-800-284-9673

Our corporate mission:

Inspire to Integrity

Our declared values:

We give to all of life as life has given us.

We honor all relationships.

Trust and stewardship are integral
to fulfilling dreams.

Collaboration is essential to create miracles.

Creativity and aesthetics nourish the soul.

Unlimited thinking is fundamental.

Living your passion is vital.

Joy and humor open our hearts to growth.

It is important to remind ourselves of love.

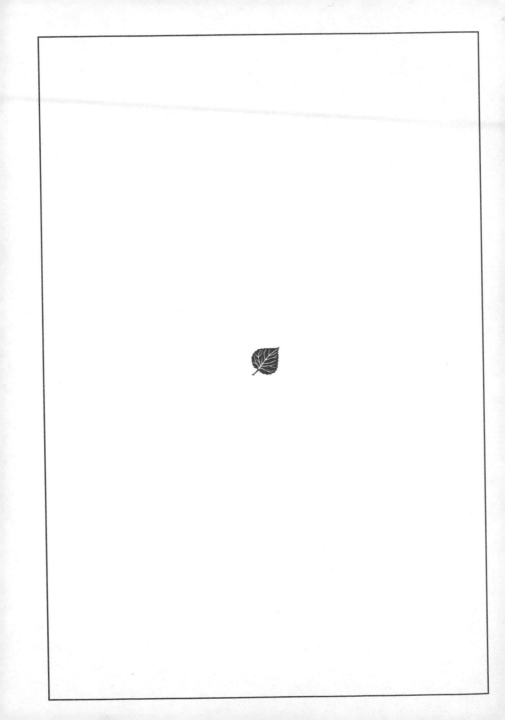

mystery

caring

human

sacrifice

playful

fair

humor

influence

generous

prote

kind

loving

inspiring

strength

respect